AUDIO
ACCESS
INCLUDED

PLAYBACK+
Speed • Pitch • Balance • Loop

Flute

CHRISTMAS CLASSICS

Audio arrangements by Peter Deneff

To access audio visit:
www.halleonard.com/mylibrary

Enter Code
2981-5388-5970-5854

ISBN 978-1-4950-7054-9

HAL•LEONARD®
CORPORATION
7777 W. BLUEMOUND RD. P.O. BOX 13819 MILWAUKEE, WI 53213

In Australia Contact:
Hal Leonard Australia Pty. Ltd.
4 Lentara Court
Cheltenham, Victoria, 3192 Australia
Email: ausadmin@halleonard.com.au

Visit Hal Leonard Online at
www.halleonard.com

ANGELS WE HAVE HEARD ON HIGH

FLUTE

Traditional French Carol

BRING A TORCH, JEANNETTE, ISABELLA

FLUTE

17th Century French Provençal Carol

COVENTRY CAROL

FLUTE

Traditional English Melody

FUM, FUM, FUM

FLUTE

Traditional Catalonian Carol

GO, TELL IT ON THE MOUNTAIN

FLUTE

African-American Spiritual

GOD REST YE MERRY, GENTLEMEN

FLUTE

Traditional English Carol

HERE WE COME A-CAROLING

FLUTE

Traditional

THE HOLLY AND THE IVY

FLUTE

18th Century English Carol

I SAW THREE SHIPS

FLUTE

Traditional English Carol

JINGLE BELLS

FLUTE

Words and Music by
J. PIERPONT

O COME, ALL YE FAITHFUL

FLUTE

Music by JOHN FRANCIS WADE

O HOLY NIGHT

FLUTE

French Words by PLACIDE CAPPEAU
English Words by JOHN S. DWIGHT
Music by ADOLPHE ADAM

SILENT NIGHT

FLUTE

Words by JOSEPH MOHR
Music by FRANZ X. GRUBER

STILL, STILL, STILL

FLUTE

Salzburg Melody, c.1819

WHAT CHILD IS THIS?

FLUTE

16th Century English Melody